Time to try....

VEGAN

CookNation

Time to try...VEGAN

ISBN 978-1-912155-84-2

Cover image under license from Shutterstock

Disclaimer

Except for use in any review, the reproduction or utilisation of this work in whole or in part in any form by any electronic, mechanical or other means, now known or hereafter invented, including xerography, photocopying and recording, or in any information storage or retrieval system, is forbidden without the permission of the publisher.

This book is sold subject to the condition that it shall not, by way of trade or otherwise, be lent, resold, hired out or otherwise circulated without the prior consent of the publisher in any form of binding or cover other than that in which it is published and without a similar condition including this condition being imposed on the subsequent purchaser.

This book is designed to provide information on vegan meals. Some recipes may contain nuts or traces of nuts. Those suffering from any allergies associated with nuts should avoid any recipes containing nuts or nut based oils.

This information is provided and sold with the knowledge that the publisher and author do not offer any legal or other professional advice.
In the case of a need for any such expertise consult with the appropriate professional.
This book does not contain all information available on the subject, and other sources of recipes are available.
Every effort has been made to make this book as accurate as possible. However, there may be typographical and or content errors. Therefore, this book should serve only as a general guide and not as the ultimate source of subject information.
This book contains information that might be dated and is intended only to educate and entertain.
The author and publisher shall have no liability or responsibility to any person or entity regarding any loss or damage incurred, or alleged to have incurred, directly or indirectly, by the information contained in this book.

CONTENTS

15 Delicious Dinners 35

10 Superfood Soups 51

INTRODUCTION

Plant based diets have never been more popular

So you've decided it's Time To Try a Vegan approach to eating

Plant based diets have never been more popular and with so many health benefits attributed to this healthier way of eating you have made a life enhancing choice.

Aside from the positive impact you will be making to the environment and animal welfare you'll notice that a vegan diet which omits processed foods will make you feel better and have more energy. By cutting out meat, animal fats and dairy produce your body will respond and you'll begin to improve your health and naturally lose weight. A vegan diet over time will help you to stick with the body shape and mass that suits you best.

To begin your vegan adventure first and foremost you'll need to understand what a vegan diet consists of. Like vegetarians, vegans don't eat meat or fish. Where the diet goes further is that vegans also don't eat any food that is produced from a live or dead animal. This includes eggs, milk, butter, cheese, yogurt and any foodstuffs made with any such ingredients.

So what do vegans eat?

In basic terms it's a diet that consists of plant-derived foods. Vegetables, fruits, grains, seeds and nuts are central to the vegan diet, and from these come a surprising variety of tasty, nutritious and healthy meals.

However simply cutting all animal based foods from your diet is not the whole answer. A balanced diet is important and you'll need to pay attention to make sure you still get all the nutrients your body needs - which is where our balanced recipes can help. Today most soya milks, nut milks and cereals are fortified with Vitamin B12. Also nutritional yeast is another excellent source of this and other vital vitamins.

Other important nutrients which vegans can sometimes lack are iron, protein, calcium, and omega 3; all of which can be found in natural plant-based foods and in fortified cereals and milks.

IRON
sources

sesame seeds, pumpkin seeds, nuts, bulgur, tofu, dried fruit quinoa, barley, oats and rice

PROTEIN
sources

Protein sources: kale, hemp seeds, nuts, tofu, quinoa, lentils and beans.

CALCIUM
sources

broccoli, kale, fennel, sesame seeds, oranges, blackcurrants, apricots

OMEGA 3
sources

walnuts, chia seeds, flax seeds, hemp seeds, cabbages, broccoli and kale, cauliflower, beans, berries, cloves, mangoes, melons.

This collection of beginner's recipes should help you start on the right track to enjoying a vegan diet. We've included quick and easy meals, snacks, soups and smoothies to enjoy which, along with some desserts too, will help complement your new way of eating and open a whole new world of culinary delights.

About CookNation

CookNation is the leading publisher of innovative and practical recipe books for the modern, health conscious cook.

CookNation titles bring together delicious, easy and practical recipes with their unique no nonsense approach - making cooking for diets and healthy eating fast, simple and fun.

With a range of #1 best-selling titles - from the innovative 'Skinny' calorie-counted series, to the 5:2 Diet Recipes collection - CookNation recipe books prove that 'Diet' can still mean 'Delicious'!

Visit **www.bellmackenzie.com** to browse the full catalogue.

9

Energy Packing BREAKFASTS

SERVES 2

Hummus and Avocado Toast

Time to try... VEGAN

Ingredients

- 2 slices whole grain bread
- 250g/9oz hummus
- 1 avocado
- A few slivers of red onion
- Salt & pepper

Method

1 Toast the bread.

2 Peel, stone and thinly slice the avocado.

3 Spread the hummus over each slice. Arrange the avocado slices on the top and scatter with onion slivers. Season with salt and pepper, and serve.

Chefs Note....

You can also mash the avocado, and either leave it sitting on top of the hummus or mix the two together.

SERVES 2

Eggless French Toast

Time to try...

VEGAN

Ingredients

- 4 thick slices day-old ciabatta bread
- 250ml/1 cup almond milk
- 1 tbsp maple syrup, plus more for serving
- 2 tbsp whole wheat flour
- 1 tbsp nutritional yeast
- 1 tsp ground cinnamon
- ¼ tsp ground nutmeg
- Pinch salt
- 1 tsp coconut oil

Method

1 In a wide, shallow dish, whisk together the almond milk, maple syrup, flour, nutritional yeast, cinnamon, nutmeg and salt.

2 Dip the bread into the mixture so that both sides are well coated.

3 Heat the coconut oil in a large frying pan. Drop in the bread slices and cook for a few minutes on each side, until golden brown.

4 If you need to fry it in batches, keep warm in the oven while you cook the rest.

Chefs Note....

Delicious on its own, or served with fresh fruit slices, a sprinkling of icing sugar or maple syrup.

SERVES 1

Breakfast Pancake

Time to try... VEGAN

Ingredients

- 50g/2oz gram flour
- ¼ tsp garlic powder
- ¼ tsp baking powder
- Pinch chilli flakes
- Salt & pepper
- 60ml/¼ cup water
- 1 spring onion, finely chopped
- ½ red pepper, de-seeded & finely chopped
- Non-stick cooking spray

Method

1 Preheat a frying pan over medium heat.

2 In a bowl, mix together the gram flour, garlic powder, baking powder and chilli flakes. Season well with salt and pepper. Add the water and whisk until smooth and bubbly. Stir in the spring onion and pepper.

3 Spray the pan with non-stick oil. Pour in the batter and tip to spread it quickly and evenly over the pan.

4 Cook for 5-6 minutes, until the pancake is firm and your spatula slides easily under it. Turn it and cook for another 5 minutes or so until golden brown.

5 Serve topped with fresh fruit, hummus, or cashew cream.

Chefs Note....

This filling pancake should easily keep hunger at bay until lunchtime.

SERVES 2

Porridge with Pomegranate

Time to try...
VEGAN

Ingredients

- 250ml/1 cup almond milk
- 200g/7oz blueberries
- ½ tbsp maple syrup
- 2 tbsp chia seeds
- 100g/3½oz jumbo oats
- 1 kiwi fruit, peeled & sliced
- 50g/2oz pomegranate seeds
- 2 tsp mixed seeds

Method

1 Use a blender to combine together the milk, blueberries and maple syrup until the milk turns purple.

2 In a bowl, mix the chia seeds and oats. Stir in the blueberry milk and leave everything to soak together for 5 minutes or so, stirring occasionally.

3 When the liquid is absorbed, and the mixture thickens, stir once more and divide the porridge between two bowls. Place the kiwi slices on top, and then sprinkle on the seeds.

Chefs Note....
Pomegranate seeds are packed with vitamins C and K, fibre and potassium.

No Bake Breakfast Bars

MAKES 6 BARS

Time to try... VEGAN

Ingredients

- 2 tbsp coconut oil
- 60ml/¼ cup maple syrup or golden syrup
- ¼ tsp salt
- 1 tsp vanilla extract
- ½ tsp ground cardamom
- ¼ tsp ground cinnamon
- Pinch nutmeg
- 75g/3oz oats
- 50g/2oz almonds, sliced
- 2 tbsp sunflower seeds
- 2 tbsp pumpkin seeds
- 1 tbsp chia seeds
- 125g/4oz chopped dried cranberries

Method

1. In a pan, melt the coconut oil and stir in the syrup, salt, vanilla and spices.
2. When the mixture grows foamy, lower the heat and stir in the oats, nuts and seeds until all are thoroughly coated. Fold in the dried cranberries. Cook for another minute or two.
3. Meanwhile, line a dish with baking parchment, leaving the sides long. Scrape the mixture out into the dish and spread it out evenly with the back of a spoon.Wrap the parchment over the top of the granola and press it hard to pack it down.
4. Put it in fridge for at least 2 hours, or preferably overnight.
5. Remove the granola from the parchment and cut it into bars.
6. Store in the fridge in an airtight container for up to 2 weeks.

Chefs Note....
Chia seeds are particularly high in protein, fibre, antioxidants, and calcium.

MAKES 1 LOAF

Banana Loaf

Time to try...

VEGAN

Ingredients

- 3 tbsp chia seeds
- 6 tbsp water
- 120ml/½ cup olive oil
- 100g/3½oz brown sugar
- 2 medium bananas, peeled & mashed
- 60ml/¼ cup black coffee
- 125g/4oz white flour
- 125g/4oz wholemeal flour
- ½ tsp salt
- 2 tsp baking powder
- 1 tsp ground cinnamon
- 1 tsp allspice

Method

1 Preheat the oven to 180C/350F/Gas4. Line a loaf tin with parchment.

2 In a bowl, whisk together the chia seeds and water.

3 In another bowl whisk together the olive oil and sugar until fluffy. Stir in the chia seed mixture, mashed bananas and coffee.

4 Sieve in the flours, salt, baking powder and spices, and fold gently together.

5 Turn the mixture into the loaf tin and bake in the oven for 30-40 minutes or until brown on top and a skewer comes out clean.

Chefs Note....
A couple of slices make a delicious and filling breakfast. Chia seeds and banana add protein, fibre and minerals.

Potato Hash

SERVES 4

Time to try...
VEGAN

Ingredients

- 3 medium potatoes, peeled & diced
- 1 large sweet potato, peeled & diced
- 1 tbsp onion granules
- 1 tbsp garlic powder
- 1 tsp dried thyme
- 2 tsp sea salt
- 1 tsp freshly ground black pepper
- 60ml/¼ cup olive oil, plus 1 tsp
- 1 medium onion, peeled & diced
- 3 cloves garlic, crushed
- Salt & pepper

Method

1 Preheat the oven to 230C/450F/Gas8

2 In a casserole dish, stir the potatoes and sweet potatoes together with the onion and garlic powders, thyme, salt, pepper and 60ml olive oil.

3 Bake in the oven for 40-50 minutes, stirring every 20 minutes or so, until the potatoes are crispy.

4 Meanwhile, heat 1 tsp olive oil in a frying pan, and sauté the diced onion and garlic for 5-6 minutes until soft and golden. Season with salt and pepper.

5 When the potatoes are done, remove the dish from the oven and stir in the onion mixture to serve.

Chefs Note....

Potatoes make a great, tasty breakfast for a winter morning – no fat, low in calories and high in vitamin C.

MAKES 12 MUFFINS

Breakfast Muffins

Time to try...
VEGAN

Ingredients

- 100g/3½oz muesli, plus 50g/2oz
- 50g/2oz light soft brown sugar
- 165g/5½oz plain flour
- 1 tsp baking powder
- 250ml/1 cup sweetened soy milk
- 1 apple, peeled, cored & grated
- 2 tbsp olive oil
- 2 tbsp almond butter, plus 1 tbsp
- 4 tbsp Demerara sugar
- 50g/2oz pecan nuts, roughly chopped

Method

1 Preheat the oven to 200C/400F/Gas6. Line a muffin tray with paper cases.

2 In a bowl, stir together 100g/3½oz muesli, the light brown sugar, flour and baking powder.

3 In a jug, mix the soy milk, apple, oil and 2 tbsp almond butter. Pour it into the dry mixture in the bowl and stir well.

4 Divide the mixture evenly between the paper cases.

5 In another bowl, combine the rest of the muesli with the Demerara sugar, and 1 tbsp almond butter. Stir in the pecans, and then spoon a little over each muffin.

6 Bake in the oven for 25-30 mins or until the muffins are risen and golden.

7 The muffins will keep for 2-3 days in an airtight container or freeze for one month. Refresh in the oven before serving.

Chefs Note....

Feel free to use your favourite nut milk instead of soy milk, and any nut butter will do in place of almond.

SERVES 1

Strawberry Quinoa

Time to try...
VEGAN

Ingredients

- 125ml/½ cup water
- 40g/1½oz cashew nuts
- 200g/7oz fresh strawberries
- 175g/6oz quinoa, cooked

Method

1 Remove the green tops from the strawberries.

2 Blend the water, nuts and strawberries together until smooth and creamy.

3 Spoon the quinoa in your cereal bowl, and pour the strawberry milk over the top.

4 If you wish, sprinkle other fruit and nuts over the top.

Chefs Note....
Quinoa is a superfood, high in protein and important minerals such as iron and zinc.

15

Quick and Easy

LUNCHES

Time to try....

VEGAN

Red Pepper Pasta

SERVES 4

Time to try...
VEGAN

Ingredients

- 300g/11oz dried pasta
- 1 onion, peeled & chopped
- 2 cloves garlic, peeled & crushed
- 2 red peppers, de-seeded & sliced lengthwise
- Large handful basil, stemmed
- 1 tbsp extra virgin olive oil
- Salt & pepper

Method

1 Cook the pasta is salted boiling water until tender.

2 Meanwhile gently sauté the onion, garlic, red pepper, and basil for a few minutes until softened and cooked through.

3 Drain the pasta and combine with the sautéed onions and peppers.

4 Toss well, drizzle with a little extra olive oil, season to taste and serve.

Chefs Note....
Basil is a good source of calcium, iron and omega 3.

Chickpea Salad

SERVES 2

Time to try... VEGAN

Ingredients

- 400g/14oz tinned chickpeas, drained & rinsed
- 3 tbsp pickled gherkins, finely chopped
- ½ red onion, peeled & finely chopped
- 2 tbsp vegan mayonnaise
- 2 tsp mustard
- 1 tsp cider vinegar
- Salt & pepper
- 2 tsp fresh dill, chopped

Method

1 In a bowl, partially mash the chickpeas with a fork or potato masher.

2 Add the gherkins, onion, mayonnaise, mustard, vinegar and dill. Season well with salt and pepper. Stir everything together and adjust the seasoning.

3 Enjoy on its own or in a wholegrain bread sandwich!

Chefs Note....
A delicious way to eat chickpeas, which are packed with important nutrients, including protein, fibre, iron and zinc.

SERVES 4

Cauliflower Salad

Time to try... VEGAN

Ingredients

- 300g/11oz cauliflower florets
- 3 tbsp vegan mayonnaise
- 1 tsp freshly squeezed lemon juice
- ½ tsp Dijon mustard
- ½ tsp Tabasco sauce
- ¼ tsp ground turmeric
- Pinch salt
- 1 stalk celery, finely chopped
- ¼ red onion, peeled & finely chopped
- 1 tsp fresh dill, finely chopped

Method

1 Steam the cauliflower over a pan of boiling water for about 5-7 minutes or until just tender.

2 Meanwhile, in a bowl, mix together the mayonnaise, lemon juice, mustard, Tabasco, turmeric and salt.

3 When the cauliflower is ready, empty it into the bowl with the other ingredients and mash with a fork or potato masher. Stir in the celery, onion and dill.

4 Serve on toast with rocket, or in a wholemeal bread sandwich.

Chefs Note....

A fantastic vegan alternative to egg mayonnaise sandwiches!

SERVES 1

Vegetable Wrap

Time to try...
VEGAN

Ingredients

- 1 medium carrot, peeled & grated
- 75g/3oz red cabbage, finely shredded
- 2 spring onions, thinly sliced
- 1 courgette, grated
- Handful basil leaves
- 5 green olives, pitted & halved
- ½ tsp English mustard powder
- 2 tsp olive oil
- 1 tbsp cider vinegar
- 1 large tortilla

Method

1 Tip everything except the tortilla into a large bowl and combine well.

2 Place the tortilla on a sheet of foil and pile the filling along one side. Roll the tortilla from the filling side, folding in the sides as you go along. Fold the foil over at the ends to keep everything inside the wrap.

3 When you're ready to eat, cut the wrap in half.

Chefs Note....
Try also with a little peanut butter spread on the tortilla.

Pasta with Broccoli

SERVES 2

Time to try... VEGAN

Ingredients

- 750ml/3 cups water
- 200g/7oz dried whole wheat pasta
- 2 tbsp plain flour
- 1 tsp garlic powder
- ½ tsp onion granules
- ¼ tsp Dijon mustard
- 1½ tbsp freshly squeezed lemon juice
- Salt & pepper
- ½ head broccoli, cut into florets
- 4 tbsp nutritional yeast

Method

1 Pour the water into a large pan and stir in the pasta, flour, garlic and onion powders, mustard and lemon juice. Season well with salt and pepper. Cover and bring to the boil, then reduce the heat and simmer for 5 minutes, stirring frequently.

2 Add the broccoli and cook for another 3-5 minutes, until the pasta is al dente.

3 Take the pan off the heat, and stir in the nutritional yeast. Leave it to rest for a couple of minutes and then serve.

Chefs Note....

The nutritional yeast will give this dish a lovely cheesy flavour. It will also give you a protein boost, but for higher iron content, make sure you buy fortified yeast.

SERVES 2

Mediterranean Tart

Time to try... VEGAN

Ingredients

- 400g/14oz mix of Mediterranean vegetables (peppers, courgettes, tomatoes, aubergines)
- 2 tbsp olive oil
- 1 tbsp fresh basil, chopped
- 1 sheet vegan puff pastry
- 2 tbsp hummus

Method

1 Preheat the oven to 220C/425F/Gas7.

2 Tip all the vegetables into a roasting tin. Drizzle on the oil and sprinkle the chopped basil over the top.

3 Roast in the oven for 20-25 minutes or until the vegetables are tender.

4 Meanwhile, roll out the pastry sheet to make one large tart or two smaller ones. Prick with a fork. Place the pastry on a baking sheet and bake in the oven for 15-20 minutes.

5 When it's ready, remove it from the oven and spread with hummus. Spoon the roasted vegetables over the top, and serve.

Chefs Note....
Feel free to vary the vegetables you use according to what you have or what you like best! Delicious either hot or cold.

SERVES 1

Bean and Mango Salad

Time to try... VEGAN

Ingredients

- 200g/7oz vegan coleslaw
- 125g/4oz fresh, ripe mango, peeled and diced
- 75g/3oz tinned black beans, rinsed
- 2 tbsp pumpkin seeds
- ½ red onion, finely chopped
- 1 tbsp rice vinegar
- 2 tsp olive oil
- 8 large lettuce leaves

Method

1 In a bowl, mix together the coleslaw, mango, black beans, pumpkin seeds, onion, vinegar and oil.

2 Spread the lettuce leaves out on a plate to make a "bed", and serve the mango and bean mixture on top.

Chefs Note....

If you have time, make your own coleslaw from finely shredded cabbage, carrot and spring onions with a little vegan mayo.

SERVES 2

Roasted Cauliflower and Broccoli Salad

Time to try...
VEGAN

Ingredients

- 200g/7oz broccoli florets
- 200g/7oz cauliflower florets
- 2 tbsp olive oil
- 250g/9oz cooked quinoa
- 2 cooked beetroots, sliced
- Handful baby spinach
- 10 walnuts, toasted and chopped
- 2 tbsp tahini
- 3 tbsp hummus
- 1 lemon, ½ juiced, ½ cut into wedges
- 1 tbsp water

Method

1 Preheat the oven to 200C/400F/Gas6.

2 Place the broccoli and cauliflower in a roasting tin. Drizzle the oil over the top and add a pinch of salt.

3 Roast in the oven for about 25 minutes or until tender, then allow to cool completely.

4 Divide the quinoa between two bowls. Arrange the beetroot slices on top, then the spinach leaves, and the roasted cauliflower and broccoli. Scatter the walnuts over the top.

5 In a small bowl, stir together the tahini, hummus, lemon juice and water. When you're ready to eat, drizzle this dressing over each bowl and serve with the lemon wedges.

Chefs Note....

You can roast the vegetables the night before and leave them to cool until the next day when you're ready for lunch.

SERVES 1

Noodle Bowl

Time to try... VEGAN

Ingredients

- 75g/3oz rice noodles
- 1 tbsp toasted sesame oil
- 1 tbsp peanut butter
- 1 tbsp brown sugar
- Dash lime juice
- ½ tsp freshly grated ginger
- ½ tbsp soy sauce
- ¼ tsp Tabasco sauce
- ½ carrot, shredded into fine julienne strips
- 1 spring onion, chopped
- 50g/2oz extra firm tofu, dried and cubed

Method

1 Cook the noodles according to packet instructions until tender.

2 Meanwhile make a peanut dressing by whisking together the sesame oil, peanut butter, brown sugar, lime juice, ginger, soy sauce and Tabasco. Whisk in a tbsp water if the dressing is too thick.

3 Once noodles are cooked, drain and rinse them in cold water. Pat them dry with kitchen towel, then put them in a serving bowl.

4 Add the carrots, spring onion and tofu to a serving bowl. Drizzle the peanut dressing over the top. Scatter with basil and a drop of sriracha if desired.

Chefs Note....
If you wish to substitute the peanut butter, use tahini instead.

SERVES 1

Kale Pesto Whole Wheat Rolls

Time to try...
VEGAN

Ingredients

- 75g/3oz fresh curly kale
- 50g/2oz walnuts
- 1 clove garlic, peeled
- 3 tbsp nutritional yeast
- 7 tbsp olive oil
- 1 tsp dried Italian herb seasoning
- Salt & pepper
- 200g/7oz smoked tofu, cut into strips
- 1 small courgette, sliced
- 1 medium carrot, spiralized
- 2 whole wheat rolls
- Lettuce leaves

Method

1 To make a kale pesto, blend together the kale, walnuts, garlic, nutritional yeast, 5 tbsp olive oil, Italian seasoning, salt and pepper, until smooth.

2 In a pan, heat 1 tbsp olive oil and fry the tofu for about 2-3 minutes on each side until it is brown and crispy. Set it aside.

3 Heat the last tbsp olive oil and sauté the courgette for another 3 minutes or so. Season with salt & pepper.

4 Cut the rolls in half and spread the pesto generously on both sides. Add the lettuce leaves on each roll, then divide the tofu, carrot, and courgette between them.

Chefs Note....
Walnuts are rich in omega 3, vitamins and minerals.

SERVES 2

Tomato and Avocado Salad with Ciabatta

Time to try... VEGAN

Ingredients

- 800g/1¾lb ripe fresh tomatoes, roughly chopped
- Salt & pepper
- 1 clove garlic, peeled & crushed
- 1 tbsp capers, drained & rinsed
- 1 ripe avocado, peeled, stoned & chopped
- 1 red onion, peeled & finely sliced
- 175g/6oz ciabatta, cut into bite-sized chunks
- 4 tbsp olive oil
- 2 tbsp red wine vinegar
- Handful basil leaves

Method

1 Place the tomatoes in a bowl. Season well with salt and pepper. Mix in the garlic, capers, avocado and onion.

2 Place the ciabatta chunks in a large serving bowl. Drizzle on half the olive oil and half the vinegar. Season.

3 When you're ready to eat, pour the tomatoes and their juices over the bread. Sprinkle with the basil leaves and the remaining oil and vinegar. Toss and serve immediately.

Chefs Note....
Any crusty bread will do in place of ciabatta.

SERVES 4

Layered Vegan Sushi Box

Time to try... VEGAN

Ingredients

- Juice from ½ lemon
- 250g/9oz rice, cooked & cooled
- ¼ tsp freshly grated ginger
- 125g/4oz carrot, peeled & sliced
- ½ cucumber, cut into thin strips
- 1 spring onion, chopped
- 1 sheets sushi nori, torn into small pieces

Method

1 Pour the lemon juice over the rice and stir in the ginger.

2 In a small square lunch container, take turns layering the rice, carrot, cucumber, onion and nori to create a tasty lunchtime layered salad.

Chefs Note....

Nori – toasted seaweed – is a good source of vitamin C and will also boost your vitamin A, potassium and magnesium.

SERVES 2-3

Spinach Salad with Lentils and Quinoa

Time to try... VEGAN

Ingredients

- 1 tbsp apple sauce
- 2 tbsp balsamic vinegar
- 1 tbsp fresh lemon juice
- 1 tbsp Dijon mustard
- Salt & pepper
- 250g/9oz cooked lentils
- 250g/9oz cooked quinoa
- ¼ red onion, peeled & finely chopped
- 2 clementines or satsumas, peeled & broken into segments
- 1 avocado, peeled, stoned & diced
- 100g/3½oz fresh chopped tomatoes
- ¼ cup fresh parsley
- ¼ cup raw pecans
- 4 handfuls fresh spinach

Method

1 In a small bowl or jug, whisk together the apple sauce, balsamic vinegar, lemon juice and mustard. Season with salt and pepper. Set aside.

2 In a larger bowl, combine all the other ingredients, except the spinach.

3 When you're ready to eat, place a handful of spinach into each bowl. Spoon the lentil mixture on top of the leaves, and drizzle the apple and balsamic dressing over all.

Chefs Note....
This delicious and filling salad provides plenty of protein, iron, calcium and zinc.

SERVES 4

Green Bean Salad

Time to try...
VEGAN

Ingredients

- 1½ tbsp olive oil
- 1 large clove garlic, peeled & thinly sliced
- ½ tbsp balsamic vinegar
- 1½ tbsp fresh mint, chopped
- Salt & pepper
- 300g/11oz green beans, cooked

Method

1 In a small pan, heat 1 tbsp of the oil and fry the garlic until it's crisp. Empty the garlic and oil into a bowl and allow to cool.

2 When you're ready to eat, combine the rest of the oil with the vinegar and mint in a small bowl, and season with salt and pepper to make a dressing

3 Pour the dressing over the beans and toss. Tip them into a serving bowl and sprinkle the garlic and oil over the top.

Chefs Note....
For a workday lunch, the beans can be cooked and the garlic fried the night before.

MAKES 6 PIES

Easy Veggie Pies

Time to try...

VEGAN

Ingredients

- 500g/1lb2oz frozen puff pastry, de-frosted
- 500g/1lb2oz frozen Mediterranean Vegetables
- 400g/14oz can chickpeas, drained & rinsed
- 1 tbsp fresh coriander, chopped
- Salt & pepper
- 150g/5oz hummus
- Soya milk, to glaze the pastry

Method

1 Preheat the oven to 220C/425F/Gas7.

2 Place the vegetables on a baking tray and cook in the oven for 25-30 minutes.

3 Allow the vegetables to cool for a few minutes, then tip them into a bowl and stir in the chickpeas and coriander. Season with salt and pepper.

4 Roll out the pastry and use a pastry cutter to cut out circles. Place half the pastry circles on a baking tray. Spread a thick layer of hummus over each, leaving the edges clear.

5 Spoon the vegetable mixture on top of the hummus. Place the remaining pastry circles on top, stretching them so they hang over the vegetables. Press down the edges, and crimp with a fork. Cut a slit in each pie then brush with a little soya milk.

6 Bake in the oven for 30-35 minutes or until golden and cooked through.

Chefs Note....

Delicious hot or cold, these make a filling and nourishing lunch. Feel free to roast fresh vegetables instead of frozen, if you have the time!

15

Delicious

DINNERS

Time to try....

VEGAN

SERVES 4

Lemon and Parsley Pasta

Time to try...
VEGAN

Ingredients

- 350g/12oz vegan tagliatelle
- 500ml/2 cups unsweetened almond milk
- 125g/4oz soy cream cheese
- 3 tbsp blanched almonds, sliced
- 3 tbsp nutritional yeast, + more for sprinkling
- 1 tsp freshly grated lemon zest
- Salt & pepper
- 2 tbsp olive oil
- 3 cloves garlic, peeled & finely chopped
- 4 tbsp fresh parsley, chopped

Method

1 Cook the pasta in salted boiling water until tender.

2 Meanwhile in your blender or food processor, blend together the soy milk, cream cheese, almonds, nutritional yeast, and lemon zest until smooth. Season well with salt and pepper.

3 Heat the oil in a large pan and fry the garlic for about a minute, until it starts to soften. Add the blended soy milk mixture and a little the cooking liquid from the pasta pan. Bring to a gentle simmer and cook, stirring, for a few minutes, until it's thick and creamy.

4 Add the cooked tagliatelle and parsley to the sauce. Toss well.

5 Divide the tagliatelle between 4 bowls. Scatter a little nutritional yeast over each and add some freshly ground black pepper.

Chefs Note....

This will work well with any vegan pasta shape you prefer.

SERVES 4

Cucumber Salad with Quinoa and Tofu

Time to try... VEGAN

Ingredients

- 60ml/¼ cup red wine vinegar
- 60ml/¼ cup Thai sweet chilli sauce
- 1 tbsp olive oil
- Pinch salt
- ½ red onion, peeled & finely sliced
- 400g/14oz extra-firm tofu, sliced & squeezed dry
- 1 cucumber, chopped
- 3 tbsp corn starch
- 2 tbsp vegetable oil
- 175g/6oz quinoa, cooked
- 2 tbsp roasted cashew nuts, halved
- Freshly picked parsley sprigs, to garnish

Method

1 In a small jug or bowl, whisk together the red wine vinegar, Thai chilli sauce and olive oil. Season with salt.

2 Tip the onion slices and cucumber into a bowl, and drizzle on about half the chilli dressing. Stir it up.

3 Lightly coat the tofu in corn starch. Heat the vegetable oil in a frying pan. Add the tofu and fry for about 2 minutes on each side, until it's golden brown all over. Drain it on kitchen towel.

4 Divide the quinoa among 4 bowls. Spoon on the cucumber and onion salad. Scatter the roasted cashew nuts over the top. Add the tofu and serve garnished with parsley. Drizzle on the rest of the dressing to taste.

Chefs Note....

Tofu is an important part of the vegan diet, being rich in protein, iron, calcium and zinc.

SERVES 4

Slow Cooker Sweet Potato Curry

Time to try...
VEGAN

Ingredients

- 3 tbsp olive oil
- 2 onions, peeled & sliced
- 2 cloves garlic, peeled & crushed
- 1 tsp freshly grated ginger
- 1 tsp paprika
- ½ tsp Cayenne pepper
- 1 red chilli, deseeded & sliced
- 1 red pepper, deseeded & sliced
- 200g/7oz red cabbage, shredded
- 750g/1lb11oz sweet potatoes, peeled & chopped
- 200g/7oz passata
- 250ml/1 cup coconut milk
- 1½ tbsp peanut butter
- Salt & pepper

Method

1 Turn on your slow cooker to warm.

2 In a large frying pan, heat 1 tbsp olive oil. Sauté the onions for about 10 minutes until they're soft. Stir in the garlic, ginger, paprika and Cayenne pepper. Cook for another minute, then tip it all into the slow cooker.

3 Return the pan to the heat and add another 1 tbsp oil. Add the chilli, red pepper and cabbage, and cook for about 5 minutes. Empty the pan into the slow cooker.

4 Heat the rest of the oil and fry the sweet potatoes for around 5 minutes, then tip them into the slow cooker, too.

5 Pour the passata and the coconut milk into the slow cooker and stir everything together.Cover and cook on Low for 6-8 hours, until the sweet potatoes are tender.

6 Stir in the peanut butter, and season to taste.

7 Serve over cooked rice, quinoa or couscous and garnish with freshly chopped coriander.

Chefs Note....

If you don't have a slow cooker, use a large pan instead, and cook, covered, on low heat for an hour, stirring frequently to prevent sticking.

SERVES 4

Black Beans with Kale and Avocado

Time to try... VEGAN

Ingredients

- 125g/4oz kale, thick stems removed, chopped
- Juice of 3 limes
- 3 tbsp olive oil
- ½ red chilli, de-seeded & finely chopped
- ½ tsp ground cumin
- ¼ tsp salt
- 1 avocado, peeled, stoned & roughly sliced
- 125g/4oz salsa
- 3 tbsp fresh coriander leaves
- 1 tbsp olive oil
- 1 shallot, peeled & finely chopped
- 3 cloves garlic, peeled & crushed
- 2 x 400g/14oz tinned black beans, rinsed & drained
- ¼ tsp chili powder
- 750g/1lb 11oz cooked rice (from 225g/8oz raw)

Method

1 In a large bowl, stir together the juice squeezed from 2 limes, 2 tbsp olive oil, the chopped, cumin and salt. Tip in the kale, toss and leave to marinate.

2 Meanwhile, blend together the avocado, salsa, coriander and remaining lime juice until smooth. Set aside.

3 Heat the remaining olive oil in a pan. Sauté the shallot and garlic for around 5 minutes then add the beans and chilli powder. Cook for another 5 minutes until the beans are thoroughly warmed.

4 Divide the cooked rice between 4 bowls. Arrange the beans and the kale salad on top and add the avocado salsa verde to each.

5 Serve and enjoy!

Chefs Note....

One of the tastiest ways to eat kale, a great source of vitamins, protein and calcium.

SERVES 4

Baked Sweet Potatoes with Chickpeas

Time to try...

VEGAN

Ingredients

- 400g/14oz tinned chickpeas, rinsed & drained
- 1 tbsp olive oil
- 4 large sweet baking potatoes scrubbed & halved lengthwise
- ½ tsp ground cumin
- ½ tsp ground coriander
- ½ tsp ground cinnamon
- ½ tsp paprika
- 3 tbsp hummus
- Juice of ½ lemon
- 3 tsp fresh dill, chopped
- 3 cloves garlic, peeled & crushed
- Splash unsweetened almond milk to thin
- Fresh tomato, sliced, to garnish
- Sprigs fresh parsley, to garnish

Method

1 Preheat the oven to 200C/400F/Gas6. Line a baking tray with foil.

2 Tip the chickpeas onto the baking tray and drizzle ½ tbsp olive oil over the top. Stir them around to coat.

3 Rub the sweet potatoes with the rest of the olive oil and arrange them face down on the same baking tray. Bake them in the oven for about 30 minutes or until the potatoes are tender and the chickpeas are golden brown.

4 Meanwhile, in a bowl, whisk together the hummus, lemon juice, dill and garlic. Add a splash of almond milk to prevent the sauce becoming too thick.

5 When they're baked, place the potatoes on 4 plates, flesh-side up. Lightly mash the insides, then pour on the chickpeas and the sauce. Serve immediately, garnished with slices of tomato and sprigs of fresh parsley.

Chefs Note....

Add salt and pepper to taste, though you'll probably find the seasoning just right.

SERVES 4

Walnut and Mushroom Burgers

Time to try...
VEGAN

Ingredients

- 450g/1lb Portobello mushroom caps, chopped
- 60g/2½oz walnuts
- 1 clove garlic
- Salt & pepper
- 2 tbsp vegetable oil
- ¼ red onion, peeled & chopped
- 3 spring onions, chopped
- 2 tsp rice wine vinegar
- 175g/6oz cooked quinoa
- 60g/2½oz corn starch
- 4 wholegrain rolls

Method

1 Preheat the oven to 190C/375F/Gas5.

2 Tip the mushrooms, walnuts and garlic into a shallow baking dish. Season with salt and pepper, and toss with 1 tbsp of the oil. Spread everything out in one even layer.

3 Bake in the oven for 20 minutes, until mushrooms are tender, then leave to cool.

4 In your food processor or blender, pulse the mushroom mixture with the red onion, spring onions, and rice wine vinegar until nearly smooth.

5 Scrape it out into a large bowl and stir in the quinoa and corn starch. Cover the bowl and leave in the fridge for at least 2 hours.

6 With your hands, form the mushroom mixture into 4 burgers.

7 Heat the remaining oil in a frying pan. Fry the burgers for about 10 minutes or so, until well-browned on each side. You may have to cook them in two batches.

8 Serve in the rolls with lettuce, tomato and homemade herby vegan mayonnaise.

Chefs Note....

Enjoy this hearty, filling burger with a crisp green side salad.

SERVES 4

Aubergine Curry

Time to try...
VEGAN

Ingredients

- 2 aubergines, chopped into bite sized pieces
- 3½ tbsp coconut oil
- 2 onions, peeled & chopped
- 1 tsp freshly grated ginger
- 2 cloves garlic, peeled & crushed
- 1 red chilli, deseeded & finely chopped
- 1 tsp ground turmeric
- 2 tsp ground coriander
- 3 black cardamom pods, slightly crushed
- 4 large plum tomatoes, roughly chopped
- Salt & pepper
- 250ml/1 cup organic coconut cream
- 60ml/¼ cup water
- Juice of ½ lime
- Handful fresh coriander leaves, chopped

Method

1 Preheat the oven to 190C/375FGas5.

2 Tip the aubergine into a roasting tin in a single layer and drizzle with 2½ tbsp coconut oil. Stir it around to coat. Roast in the oven for 15-20 minutes, turning the aubergine pieces after 8-10, until they are soft and golden.

3 In a suitable casserole dish, heat the remaining oil on the hob. Sauté the onions until they're soft. Add the ginger, garlic and chilli, and cook for another 2 minutes, then add the turmeric, coriander and cardamom pods. Stir for another minute, before adding the tomatoes. Season with salt and pepper.

4 Cook, stirring, until the tomatoes begin to soften, then add the coconut cream, the water and the roasted aubergines.

5 Reduce the heat and simmer for half an hour, stirring occasionally. Add the lime juice and adjust the seasoning. Stir in the coriander.

6 Serve over rice or quinoa.

Chefs Note....

Always choose brown rice over white as it is more nutritious. However quinoa contains more protein and fibre than either.

SERVES 4

Butternut Squash Fettucine

Time to try... VEGAN

Ingredients

- 2 tbsp olive oil
- 1 tbsp fresh sage, finely chopped
- Salt & pepper
- 1 butternut squash, peeled, seeded & diced
- 1 onion, peeled & chopped
- 2 cloves garlic, peeled & crushed
- Pinch chilli flakes
- 500ml/2 cups vegetable stock
- 350g/12oz whole wheat fettucine

Method

1 Heat the oil in a large frying pan. Fry the sage, stirring to coat it in the oil. When it's crispy, remove it to a bowl and sprinkle with salt. Set aside.

2 Add the squash, onion, garlic and chilli flakes to the same pan. Season with salt and pepper. Cook, stirring occasionally, for about 10 minutes, until the onion is translucent. Pour in the stock and bring to the boil.

3 Lower the heat and simmer for about 20 minutes until the squash is tender and the liquid reduces by about half.

4 Meanwhile, cook the pasta according to packet instructions. Reserve about 250ml/1 cup of the cooking liquid when you drain it.

5 When the squash mixture is ready, leave it to cool slightly, then empty the pan into your blender. Blend into a smooth puree. Season with salt and pepper.

6 Return the squash puree to the same frying pan. Stir in the fettucine and a little of the reserved cooking liquid. Heat well, tossing to coat all the pasta in the sauce. Add more of the cooking liquid as necessary. Adjust the seasoning.

7 Divide the fettucine between 4 bowls and top each with the fried sage.

Chefs Note....

Sage is packed with vitamins, iron, calcium and fibre.

SERVES 2

Pepper and Mushroom Fajitas

Time to try... VEGAN

Ingredients

- 1 tbsp coconut oil
- 1 onion, peeled & sliced
- 1 green chilli, de-seeded & finely sliced
- 1 red pepper, de-seeded & sliced
- 1 yellow pepper, de-seeded & sliced
- 1 red chilli, de-seeded & thinly sliced
- Salt & pepper
- ½ tsp ground cumin
- Pinch garlic powder
- 2 large Portobello mushroom caps, chopped
- 2 ripe avocados, peeled, stoned & chopped
- Juice of ½ lime
- 6 mini tortillas

Method

1 Preheat a frying pan along with the coconut oil.

2 Add the mushrooms, onion, chilli and peppers. Season with salt and pepper, cumin and garlic powder. Cook, stirring frequently, until softened. Cover and set aside.

3 In a bowl, mix the avocado pieces with the lime juice and a pinch of salt to taste.

4 Warm the tortillas in the microwave, then serve them with the peppers, mushrooms and guacamole.

Chefs Note....

Serve with any garnishes you like, e.g. chopped fresh coriander leaves, sliced tomatoes, salsa or a sprinkling of nutritional yeast.

SERVES 4

Cauliflower and Chickpea Flatbreads

Time to try...
VEGAN

Ingredients

- 350g/12oz cauliflower florets
- 400g/14oz tinned chickpeas, rinsed & drained
- 2 tbsp olive oil
- Salt & pepper
- 2 ripe avocados
- 2 tbsp freshly squeezed lemon juice
- 4 flatbreads, toasted
- 2 tbsp roasted salted pumpkin seeds
- Pepper sauce, to serve

Method

1 Preheat the oven to 220C/425FGas7.

2 On a large baking tray, toss the cauliflower and chickpeas with the olive oil to coat them thoroughly. Sprinkle with salt and pepper. Roast them in the oven for approx. 25 minutes, shaking once during the cooking time.

3 Meanwhile, mash the avocados with the lemon juice and a pinch of salt. Spread the mixture generously over the flatbreads. Divide the roasted cauliflower and chickpea mixture between them, and sprinkle with pumpkin seeds. Serve with a dash of pepper sauce.

Chefs Note....
If you can get them, use a packet of organic chickpeas instead of canned.

SERVES 4

Lentil and Potato Bake

Time to try...
VEGAN

Ingredients

- 2 tbsp olive oil
- 1 onion, peeled & sliced
- 300g/11oz mushrooms, sliced
- 2 cloves garlic, peeled & crushed
- 1 tsp ground cumin
- 1 tsp smoked paprika
- 450g/1lb cooked lentils
- 1 tbsp soy sauce
- 1 tbsp balsamic vinegar
- 120ml/½ cup water
- Salt & pepper
- 1 large sweet potato, scrubbed & finely sliced
- 1 large white potato, scrubbed & finely sliced
- Fresh thyme leaves, to serve

Method

1 Preheat the oven to 200C/400F/Gas6.

2 In a large pan, heat 1 tbsp oil. Fry the onion for a couple of minutes, then add the mushrooms. Cook for another 3 minutes. Add the garlic, cumin and paprika, and cook for a further minute or so.

3 Remove the pan from the heat. Stir in the cooked lentils, soy sauce, balsamic vinegar and water. Season well with salt and pepper. Pour the mixture into a casserole dish.

4 Bring a pan of water to the boil. Add the potato and sweet potato slices. Cook them for 3-4 minutes, then drain.

5 Place the potato slices on top of the lentils in the casserole dish. Brush them with the remaining oil.

6 Put the casserole dish in the oven and roast for 25-30 minutes, until the potatoes are golden brown, then scatter with the thyme to serve.

Chefs Note....

Eat plenty of lentils in your diet to boost your intake of protein and zinc.

SERVES 4

Vegetables in Peanut Sauce

Time to try... VEGAN

Ingredients

- 2 large sweet potatoes, peeled & sliced
- 1 red pepper, de-seeded & sliced
- 1 tbsp coconut oil, + 1 tsp
- ¼ tsp ground cumin
- Salt
- 275g/10oz brown rice
- 125g/4oz smooth peanut butter
- 60ml/¼ cup soy sauce
- 3 tbsp cider vinegar
- 1 tbsp agave nectar
- 1 tsp freshly grated ginger
- 2 cloves garlic, peeled & crushed
- Pinch chilli flakes
- 2 tbsp water

Method

1 Preheat the oven to 220C/425F/Gas7.

2 In a roasting tin, toss the sweet potato with 1 tbsp coconut oil and cumin and spread into a single layer. Season with salt. Roast in the oven for about 35 minutes, turning once during cooking.

3 In a separate roasting tin, toss the pepper with a tsp coconut oil. Roast in the oven for about 20 minutes, shaking up once during cooking.

4 Meanwhile cook the rice in boiling water until tender, then drain. Fluff the rice with a fork and season with salt to taste.

5 In a small bowl, whisk together the peanut butter, soy sauce, vinegar, agave, ginger, garlic, chilli and water to make a peanut sauce.

6 Divide the rice between 4 bowls. Add the roasted vegetables and drizzle the peanut sauce over the top.

Chefs Note....

If you wish, serve garnished with chopped spring onion, peanuts and coriander leaves.

SERVES 4

Easy Veggie Burgers

Time to try...
VEGAN

Ingredients

- 400g/14oz tinned chickpeas, drained & rinsed
- ½ red onion, peeled & finely chopped
- 1 courgette, grated
- 3 tbsp coriander, chopped
- 3 tbsp red wine vinegar
- 1 tbsp sriracha sauce
- 2 tbsp natural peanut butter
- 1 tsp ground cumin
- 1 tsp garlic powder
- Salt & pepper
- 75g/3oz oats
- 3 tbsp olive oil,
- 8 wholemeal rolls

Method

1 In a large bowl mash the chickpeas, then combine in all the other ingredients (apart from 1 tbsp of the olive oil).

2 With your hands, shape the mixture into 8 burgers.

3 Heat the remaining oil in a frying pan, and fry the burgers for about 4 minutes on each side or until they are piping hot.

4 Serve in rolls with plenty of crisp green salad and sliced tomatoes.

Chefs Note....

On a summer night, cook on the barbeque instead, for about 10 minutes on each side.

SERVES 2

Lentil, Squash and Spinach Stew

Time to try...
VEGAN

Ingredients

- 1 shallot, peeled & finely sliced
- 2 tsp freshly grated ginger
- 1 tbsp vegetable oil
- 1 butternut squash, peeled, de-seeded & chopped
- 250g/8oz green lentils, rinsed
- 750ml/3 cups vegetable stock
- ½ tsp ground coriander
- ¼ tsp ground cardamom
- Salt & pepper
- 550g/1¼lb baby spinach
- 1 tbsp cider vinegar

Method

1 Heat the oil in a pan. Sauté the shallot and ginger for around 5 minutes until the shallot is golden. Stir in the coriander and cardamom and cook for another minute, stirring. Add the squash, lentils and stock. Season with salt and pepper.

2 Bring to the boil, then cover and reduce the heat. Cook for around 20-30 minutes until the lentils are cooked and the squash is tender.

3 Stir in the spinach and vinegar. Adjust the seasoning and serve.

Chefs Note....

Spinach is a vegan superfood; packed with vitamins, calcium, protein and zinc.

SERVES 2

Easy Vegan Chilli

Time to try...
VEGAN

Ingredients

- 400g/14oz roasting vegetable mix
- 400g/14oz tinned kidney beans in chilli sauce
- 400g/14oz tinned chopped tomatoes
- Salt & pepper
- 250g/8oz mixed grains, e.g. Wheatberries with Quinoa and Soya

Method

1 Preheat the oven to 200C/400F/Gas6.

2 Tip the vegetables into a casserole dish and bake in the oven for 15-20 minutes.

3 Stir in the beans and tomatoes. Season with salt and pepper and return to the oven for another 10-15 minutes.

4 Meanwhile, heat the mixed grain according to packet instructions.

5 Divide the grain between 2 bowls. Pour the chilli over the top and serve.

Chefs Note....
A quick and nourishing recipe for those busy mid-week nights.

10

Superfood SOUPS

Time to try....

VEGAN

SERVES 4

Spinach and Pasta Soup

Time to try...
VEGAN

Ingredients

- 2 tbsp olive oil
- 1 onion, peeled & chopped
- 1 small carrot, peeled & diced
- 1 stalk celery, finely chopped
- 3 cloves garlic, peeled & crushed
- 1.5lt/6 cups vegetable stock
- 400g/14oz can chopped tomatoes
- 250g/8oz whole wheat pasta
- 1 tbsp fresh thyme leaves
- 1 tsp fresh oregano, chopped
- 1 tsp fresh rosemary leaves
- 900g/2lb spinach
- Salt & pepper

Method

1 Heat the oil in a large pan and sauté the onion for 5 minutes, until soft. Stir in the carrots, celery and garlic and cook for another 3 minutes or so. Pour in the chicken stock then stir in the tomatoes, pasta and herbs.

2 Bring to the boil, stirring occasionally, then lower the heat and simmer for 10 minutes, until the pasta is al dente.

3 Stir in the spinach and cook for a couple of minutes until it wilts.

4 Adjust the seasoning to taste, and serve garnished with nutritional yeast or chilli flakes.

Chefs Note....

This simple recipe makes a nourishing and filling soup. Blend before serving if you prefer a smooth consistency.

Chunky Black Bean Soup

SERVES 4

Time to try...

VEGAN

Ingredients

- 1 tbsp olive oil
- ½ onion, finely chopped
- 1 medium carrot, chopped
- 1 stalk celery, sliced
- 2 tbsp tomato puree
- 2 cloves garlic, crushed
- 1 tsp ground cumin
- 360ml/12½floz vegetable stock
- 2 x 400g/14oz cans black beans, un-drained
- 100g/3½oz sweetcorn, frozen or scraped from the cob
- Salt & pepper
- Fresh parsley and coriander leaves, to garnish

Method

1 Heat the oil in a large pan. Sauté the onion, carrot and celery for 6 to 8 minutes, until starting to brown. Stir in the tomato paste, garlic and cumin. Pour in the stock, beans and sweetcorn.

2 Bring to the boil, then cover and reduce the heat. Simmer for about half an hour, then adjust the seasoning to taste.

3 Serve garnished with fresh parsley and coriander.

Chefs Note....

Black beans are rich in protein and minerals.

SERVES 4

Lentil Curry Soup

Time to try...
VEGAN

Ingredients

- 1 tbsp olive oil
- 1 tsp freshly grated ginger
- 6 cloves garlic, peeled & finely chopped
- 1 shallot, peeled & finely chopped
- 2 large organic carrots, peeled & diced
- 2 tsp curry powder
- 1 tsp salt
- 120ml/½ cup unsweetened coconut milk, + 4 tbsp to garnish
- 1.25lt/5 cups water
- 200g/7oz red lentils, rinsed
- 125g/4oz dried cranberries
- 3 tbsp coriander leaves, chopped, to garnish

Method

1 Heat the oil in a large pan. Sauté the ginger, garlic, shallot and carrots for about 8 minutes until they soften. Stir in the curry powder and cook for another minute until you can smell it. Then stir in the salt, 120ml/½ cup coconut milk, water and lentils. Bring to the boil, then reduce the heat, cover and simmer for about 10 minutes, until the lentils and carrots are tender.

2 Let the soup cool slightly, then blend it until smooth. Alternatively, you may like to blend only half of it and leave it slightly chunkier. Leaving a few cranberries for garnish, stir in the rest.

3 Ladle the soup into bowls and swirl a tablespoon of the remaining coconut milk into each. Garnish with the reserved cranberries and coriander leaves.

Chefs Note....

For a more unusual contrasting flavour, try also with dried cherries instead of cranberries.

SERVES 2

Creamy Broccoli Soup

Time to try... VEGAN

Ingredients

- 50g/2oz cashew nuts, soaked in water
- 1 tsp extra virgin olive oil
- 1 onion, peeled & diced
- 1 stalk celery, chopped
- 2 carrots, peeled & chopped
- 2 cloves garlic, peeled & crushed
- 225g/8oz broccoli, broken into florets
- 500ml/2 cups vegetable stock, + 120ml/½ cup
- Salt and pepper

Method

1 Heat the oil in a large pan. Sauté the onion for 3 minutes or so, then add the celery and carrot and sauté for another 5 minutes. Then stir in the garlic and the broccoli and cook for another 5.

2 Add 500ml of stock, and season well with salt, and pepper. Bring to the boil, then lower the heat, cover and simmer for 15 minutes.

3 Meanwhile, drain the soaking cashew nuts and blend them together with 120ml/½ cup water until very smooth and creamy. Set aside.

4 Blend the soup into a puree, then stir in the cashew cream. Adjust the seasoning and serve.

Chefs Note....

The cashew cream adds delicious flavour and texture to the soup. Cashews are also packed with vitamins, antioxidants and minerals, including iron and zinc.

SERVES 4

Vegetable and Lentil Soup

Time to try... VEGAN

Ingredients

- 4 tbsp olive oil
- 1 onion, peeled & chopped
- 2 medium carrots, diced
- 2 stalks celery, chopped
- 2 cloves garlic, peeled & finely chopped
- 1 tsp dried oregano
- 1 bay leaf
- 1 tsp dried basil
- 1.25lt/5 cups water
- 375g/13oz dry lentils
- 400g/14oz passata
- 15g/½oz spinach, finely chopped
- Salt & pepper to taste

Method

1 Heat the oil in a large pan and sauté the onion, carrot and celery until the onion is tender. Stir in garlic, bay leaf, oregano and basil and cook for 2 minutes.

2 Pour in the water, lentils and passata. Bring to the boil, then lower the heat, cover and simmer for an hour.

3 Stir in the spinach and cook until it wilts. Season with salt and pepper to taste, and serve.

Chefs Note....

This chunky, warming soup makes a whole meal, served with warm, crusty wholemeal bread.

SERVES 1

Easy Beetroot Soup

Time to try...
VEGAN

Ingredients

- 250g/9oz cooked beetroots, roughly chopped
- 100g/3½oz cooked lentils
- 1 small apple, peeled, cored & quartered
- 1 clove garlic, crushed
- 1 tsp onion seeds, + extra to serve
- 250ml/1 cup vegetable stock

Method

1 Put all the ingredients into your blender and blitz into a puree.

2 Heat the soup on the hob or in the microwave until piping hot.

3 Pour into a bowl and scatter over some extra onion seeds.

Chefs Note....

Keep the beetroot leaves if you can, and tear them up as a garnish. Beet greens are even more nourishing than the root, being packed with iron, calcium and vitamins.

SERVES 4

Carrot and Ginger Soup

Time to try...
VEGAN

Ingredients

- 1 tbsp olive oil
- 1 onion, peeled & finely chopped
- 4 large carrots, peeled & finely chopped
- 2 apples, peeled, cored & finely chopped
- 2 tsp freshly grated ginger
- 2 tsp ground turmeric
- 750ml/3 cups vegetable stock
- Salt & pepper

Method

1 Heat the oil in a large pan and sauté onion for about 5 minutes until it begins to soften. Add the garlic and cook for another couple of minutes. Stir in the carrot, apple and ginger. Cook for a further 3-4 minutes, then stir in the turmeric.

2 Pour in the stock, and season with salt and pepper. Bring to the boil, then cover and reduce the heat. Simmer for about 20 minutes, or until the carrots are thoroughly cooked.

3 Remove the pan from the heat and blend the soup until smooth. Adjust the seasoning and reheat if necessary before you serve.

Chefs Note....
Try garnished with roasted chickpeas or kale crisps.

SERVES 4

Parsnip and Squash Soup

Time to try... VEGAN

Ingredients

- 1 tbsp olive oil
- 1 onion, peeled & chopped
- 2 parsnips, peeled & chopped
- 200g/7oz butternut squash, peeled & chopped
- 1 apple, peeled, cored & chopped
- ½ tsp ground coriander
- ½ tsp ground cumin
- 500ml/2 cups vegetable stock
- 1 tsp fresh thyme leaves
- ½ tsp fresh sage, chopped
- Salt & pepper

Method

1 Heat the oil in a large pan. Sauté the onion for 5 minutes, then add the parsnip, squash and apple. Stir in the coriander and cumin and cook for another couple of minutes until fragrant. Pour in the stock and add the herbs. Season with a little salt and pepper.

2 Bring to the boil then cover and cook for about 30 minutes, until the parsnip and squash are both tender.

3 Blend the soup until smooth. Adjust the seasoning and serve with a little cashew cream and a few chopped coriander leaves.

Chefs Note....

This delicious, warming winter soup also cooks well in a slow cooker. Simply add all the ingredients, cover and cook on Low for 6-7 hours, then blend.

SERVES 4

Simple Carrot and Coriander Soup

Time to try...
VEGAN

Ingredients

- 1 tbsp olive oil
- 3 large carrots, peeled and roughly chopped
- ½ onion, peeled & chopped
- 750ml/3 cups vegetable stock
- Handful of fresh coriander, chopped
- Salt & pepper

Method

1 Heat the oil in a large pan. Gently fry the onion and carrot for about 5 minutes until the onion softens, then pour in the vegetable stock. Stir in the coriander.

2 Bring the soup to the boil, then reduce the heat, cover and simmer for 15 minutes or so, until the carrots are very tender.

3 Let it cool a little, then blend the soup until smooth. Adjust the seasoning to taste, and serve.

Chefs Note....

Coriander leaves are packed with vitamins, calcium, zinc and iron.

SERVES 1

Easy Cream of Tomato Soup

Time to try... VEGAN

Ingredients

- 4 tomatoes, peeled & quartered
- 2 cloves garlic, crushed
- Salt & pepper
- 400ml/14floz coconut milk
- ½ tsp turmeric
- Sprig fresh parsley, to garnish

Method

1 Peel the tomatoes by immersing them in a bowl of boiling water for a minute or two.

2 Blend all the ingredients together, then heat on the hob or in the microwave.

3 Adjust the seasoning to taste, and serve, garnished with a sprig of fresh parsley.

Chefs Note....

As well as adding colour to your soup, turmeric is rich in vitamins and minerals and is a natural anti-inflammatory.

20

Vegan Vitality

SNACKS & SMOOTHIES

Time to try....

VEGAN

SERVES 1-2

Kale Crisps

Time to try... VEGAN

Ingredients

- A couple of handfuls of large whole kale leaves
- Extra virgin olive oil
- Salt & pepper
- Sprinkling nutritional yeast

Method

1 Pre-heat the oven to 150C/300F/Gas2.

2 Cut the tough central stock out of the kale leaves, to make 2 thin pieces from each leaf. Place them on a baking tray and toss them in olive oil. Spread them out so that each leaf piece is separate. Season generously with salt and pepper, and sprinkle on some nutritional yeast.

3 Bake in the oven for 15 minutes, then turn the leaves carefully. Return them to the oven for another 15 minutes. Switch off the oven and leave the kale in there to crisp and cool.

4 When cooled, enjoy as a tasty any-time snack!

Chefs Note....

High in vitamins, calcium and other minerals, kale is a wonderful natural energy booster.

MAKES 6 BARS

Date and Cacao Energy Bars

Time to try...
VEGAN

Ingredients

- 275g/10oz Medjool dates, roughly chopped
- 125g/4oz walnuts, chopped
- 100g/3½oz cacao nibs

Method

1 Line a small baking tray or large, shallow dish with parchment.

2 In a food processor, process the dates into a paste. Add the nuts and process to combine - scraping down your food processor as necessary. Add the cacao, and pulse to mix them through evenly.

3 Scrape the mixture out onto the baking tray, and shape it into an even, compact rectangle, about ½-inch thick.

4 Refrigerate for at least half an hour, then cut it into bars.

Chefs Note....
Substitute vegan dark chocolate chips for the cacao nibs. Both contain cacao, which should help reduce stress and boost energy.

MAKES 6 BARS

Blackcurrant and Beetroot Bars

Time to try... VEGAN

Ingredients

- 1 beetroot, cooked, peeled & quartered
- 3 bananas, each broken into 3 pieces
- 175g/6oz oats, + 50g/2oz
- 3 tbsp maple syrup, + 1 tbsp
- 100g/3½oz almonds, chopped
- 75g/3oz blackcurrants
- 50g/2oz hazelnuts, chopped
- 50g/20z pumpkin seeds
- 60ml/¼ cup almond milk

Method

1 Preheat the oven to 180C/350F/Gas4. Line a small baking tray with parchment.

2 Blend the beetroot and bananas together until smooth. Stir in 175g/6oz oats, 3 tbsp maple syrup and the chopped almonds.

3 Scrape the mixture out onto the baking tray and spread it evenly. Bake in the oven for 8-10 minutes. Set aside.

4 In a bowl, mix together the blackcurrants, hazelnuts, pumpkin seeds, and the remaining oats and maple syrup. Stir in the almond milk. Spread the mixture over the baked layer in the baking tray.

5 Pop the tray back in the oven for another 15 minutes, then take it out and allow to cool. Cut into bars and enjoy as required.

Chefs Note....

This tasty combination of ingredients provides a massive hit of omega 3 and subsequent energy.

MAKES 10 BALLS

Nutty Energy Balls

Time to try...

VEGAN

Ingredients

- 6 Medjool dates, pitted & roughly chopped
- 75g/3oz almond butter
- 75g/3oz pistachio nuts, shelled
- 75g/3oz sesame seeds
- 1 tbsp coconut oil
- 1 tsp lime juice

Method

1 Blend the dates with the almond butter until smooth. Add the pistachios, sesame seeds, coconut oil and lime juice and blend again until everything's evenly mixed.

2 Scrape the mixture out onto a board. Use your hands to compress and roll the mixture into 10 balls.

3 Store them in an airtight container in the fridge and eat as you like.

Chefs Note....

Sweet and quick to eat, these are a delicious way to boost your energy levels during a hard day.

MAKES 15 BITES

Chia and Cherry Bites

Time to try...
VEGAN

Ingredients

- 50g/2oz dried cherries, chopped
- 50g/2oz chocolate chips
- 60g/2½oz rolled oats
- 40g/2½oz coconut flakes
- 40g/2½oz chia seeds
- 175g/6oz almond butter
- 4 tbsp maple syrup

Method

1 In a bowl, mix together the cherries, chocolate chips, oats, coconut and chia seeds. Stir in the almond butter and maple syrup until thoroughly combined.

2 Use your hands to form the mixture into about 15 bite-sized pieces.

Chefs Note....

Bite-sized treats packing a decent energy punch, largely due to the chia seeds which are rich in protein, antioxidants, calcium and omega 3.

MAKES 10 BALLS

Chocolate and Maca Energy Balls

Time to try... VEGAN

Ingredients

- 50g/2oz maca powder.
- 50g/2oz cocoa powder, plus extra to dust
- Pinch sea salt
- 1 tsp ground cinnamon
- 225g/8oz almond butter.
- Dash vanilla extract
- 1 tbsp maple syrup

Method

1 In a bowl, mix together the maca powder, cocoa, salt and cinnamon. Stir in the almond butter, vanilla and maple syrup.

2 With your (clean!) hands, roll the mixture into about 10 bite-sized balls, and dust each with cocoa powder. Chill the balls in the fridge until you need them.

Chefs Note....

Maca boosts energy and helps you handle stress. Plus it gives a pleasant nutty flavour to food, which adds to this yummy truffle.

MAKES 12 SQUARES

Apricot and Cinnamon Squares

Time to try...
VEGAN

Ingredients

- 175g/6oz Medjool dates, pitted
- 175g/6oz dried apricots
- 2 tbsp chia seeds
- ¼ tsp ground cinnamon
- 125g/4oz pumpkin seeds
- 2 tbsp vegan white chocolate chips

Method

1 Line a square baking tray or dish with parchment.

2 In a food processor, blend together the dates, apricots, chia seeds and cinnamon until the mixture forms into one chunk. Break up the chunk and add the pumpkin seeds. Pulse to chop and mix the seeds through. Break up the mixture again, add the chocolate chips and pulse a few times more.

3 Scrape the mixture out into the baking tray. Spread it evenly around the tray and press to compact.

4 Put the tray in the fridge for at least 45 minutes, or preferably overnight. Then cut into squares and store in an airtight container until you want them.

Chefs Note....

Dates help you metabolize the protein, calcium and zinc from the seeds and so boost your energy levels. The squares are also delicious – chewy, sweet and crunchy.

MAKES 12 BISCUITS

Coconut and Lemon Biscuits

Time to try...
VEGAN

Ingredients

- 300g/11oz flaked coconut
- 2 tbsp coconut oil
- 120ml/½ cup agave nectar
- 1 tsp vanilla
- Juice & zest of 1 lemon
- ¼ tsp sea salt
- 125g/4oz desiccated coconut

Method

1 In a blender or food processor, blend the flaked coconut with the coconut oil until creamy. Stir in the agave, vanilla, lemon juice and zest and the sea salt. Then, mix in the shredded coconut.

2 Scrape the mixture out onto a board and shape a spoonful at a time into little biscuits. Place them in the fridge to set, or preferably in a dehydrator if you have one for 24 hours, then enjoy!

Chefs Note....
An all-natural biscuit with energy-boosting fats.

MAKES 10 BALLS

Raspberry and Nut Energy Balls

Time to try...
VEGAN

Ingredients

- 40g/1½oz shredded coconut, + 50g/2oz
- 60g/2½oz raspberries
- 75g/3½oz almonds
- 4 Medjool dates, pitted
- 25g/1oz dried cranberries
- 60g/2½oz almond butter

Method

1 Line a baking tray or large dish with parchment. Place 40g/1½oz coconut in your food processor and process to fine crumb crumbs. Empty them into a shallow bowl and set aside.

2 Add the rest of the coconut to the food processor, along with the raspberries, almonds, dates, cranberries and almond butter. Process on high speed until the ingredients are well broken down and combined. Scrape the mixture out onto a board.

3 Roll about 1 tablespoon of the mixture into a bite sized ball. Roll the ball in the coconut crumbs to coat it all over. Place it on the baking tray. Repeat with the rest of the mixture.

4 Put the baking tray in the fridge for 2 hours before eating the balls.

Chefs Note....
Lots of fruity goodness and an energy blast in one bite.

MAKES 6 BARS

Peanut and Maple Syrup Energy Bars

Time to try...
VEGAN

Ingredients

- 3 tbsp peanut butter
- 4 tbsp maple syrup, + 2 tbsp
- 50g/2oz dark chocolate chips
- 1 tsp ground cinnamon
- ½ tsp freshly grated ginger
- 1 tbsp raisins
- 1 tbsp chia seeds
- 40g/1½oz puffed buckwheat

Method

1 Line a small square baking tray or shallow dish with parchment.

2 Heat a non-stick pan and pour in the maple syrup. Stir in the peanut butter, then reduce the heat and cook gently until they're melted together. Stir in the cinnamon, grated ginger, raisins and chia seeds.

3 Take the pan off the heat, and gently fold in the puffed buckwheat until it's thoroughly coated.

4 Turn the mixture out onto the baking tray and press down to compact as much as possible. Put the tray in the fridge to chill.

5 When chilled, cut into bars. Store the bars in an airtight container until you're ready to eat them.

Chefs Note....
These energy bars will keep in the fridge for up to 2 weeks, or in the freezer for 2 months.

SERVES 2

Blackcurrant Detox Smoothie

Time to try... VEGAN

Ingredients

- 100g/3½oz blackcurrants
- 225g/8oz kale, thick stems removed
- 1 sliced, frozen banana
- 1 tbsp flax seeds
- 250ml/1 cup blackcurrant juice

Method

1 Add the blackcurrants, kale and frozen banana to your blender. Sprinkle on the flax seeds and pour in the juice.

2 Cover and blend on High until smooth. Depending on your preference, you might want to add a splash more juice to thin the smoothie. If you prefer it sweeter, add another half banana.

3 Pour the smoothie into 2 tall glasses and drink immediately.

Chefs Note....

Especially good for those who've over-indulged, this smoothie is packed with vitamins, antioxidants, omega 3 and more.

SERVES 2

Green Mango Smoothie

Time to try...
VEGAN

Ingredients

- 250ml/1 cup coconut water
- 125ml/1 cup mango juice
- 1 tbsp freshly squeezed lemon juice
- 2 crisp green apples, cored & quartered
- 75g/3oz fresh mango, peeled & roughly chopped
- ½ avocado, peeled, stoned & halved
- 75g/3oz romaine lettuce
- 4 tbsp fresh flat leaf parsley leaves
- 4 tbsp fresh coriander leaves
- 15g/1oz fresh turmeric, peeled
- A few ice cubes
- Agave nectar to taste

Method

1 Pour the coconut water, mango juice and lemon juice into your blender. Add the fruit, lettuce, herbs and turmeric and drop in a few ice cubes.

2 Blend on High until the mixture is perfectly smooth. Taste, and add a little agave or other liquid sweetener if you wish. Drink and enjoy.

3 The smoothie will keep for up to 24 hours in the fridge.

Chefs Note....

Mangoes are regarded as a superfood, being rich in vitamins and minerals, including iron, calcium and potassium. This tasty smoothie will give you an all-round nutritional boost.

SERVES 1

Walnut and Banana Smoothie

Time to try...
VEGAN

Ingredients

- 250ml/1 cup water
- 2 tsp flaxseed oil
- 1 frozen banana
- 60g/2½oz cooked quinoa
- 1 tbsp walnuts, chopped, + extra to garnish
- 1 Medjool date, pitted
- ½ tsp pure vanilla extract
- 1 tsp ground cinnamon, + extra to garnish

Method

1 Pour the water and flaxseed oil into your blender. Add the frozen banana, quinoa, walnuts, date, vanilla and cinnamon.

2 Blend until completely smooth. Pour into a tall glass and sprinkle chopped walnuts and ground cinnamon on the top.

3 Drink at once and enjoy.

Chefs Note....

This delicious smoothie provides several of those hard-to-maintain nutrients, such as omega 3 (from the flaxseed oil and walnuts)), and protein and zinc (from the quinoa).

SERVES 2

Avocado and Spinach Smoothie

Time to try...
VEGAN

Ingredients

- 250ml/1 cup unsweetened almond milk
- 1 avocado, peeled, stoned & roughly chopped
- 1 ripe banana, broken into 3 pieces
- 1 sweet red apple, peeled, cored & roughly chopped
- 1 stalk celery, roughly chopped
- 450g/1lb spinach
- 1 tsp freshly grated ginger
- 1 tbsp chia seeds
- A few ice cubes

Method

1 Pour the almond milk into your blender. Add the fruit, celery and spinach and sprinkle in the ginger and chia seeds.

2 Drop in a few ice cubes, cover and blend on High until very smooth.

3 Pour into 2 glasses and serve.

Chefs Note....

Most commercial almond milks are fortified with calcium and vitamins A and D. The chia seeds will also boost your calcium, omega 3 and protein, while the superfood spinach contains most of the nutrients you need! AND the smoothie tastes wonderful, too!

SERVES 1

Blueberry and Maple Syrup Smoothie

Time to try... VEGAN

Ingredients

- 120ml/½ cup soy milk
- 60ml/¼ cup water
- 1 scoop vanilla protein powder
- 50g/2oz fresh or frozen blueberries
- 2 tbsp maple syrup
- 2 tsp flax seeds
- A few ice cubes

Method

1 Pour the soy milk and water into your blender. Sprinkle in the protein powder, then add the blueberries, maple syrup and flax seeds. Top with a few ice cubes.

2 Cover and blend it all together.

3 Add more ice to thicken, if you wish, and blend again.

4 Pour it into a glass and drink.

Chefs Note....

Delicious and sweet, this smoothie is also rich in protein, omega 3 and calcium. Feel free to substitute other non-dairy milk for soy, and use more milk instead of water.

SERVES 2

Date and Vanilla Nut Milk

Time to try... VEGAN

Ingredients

- 125g/4oz whole hazelnuts
- 40g/1½oz whole almonds
- 750ml/3 cups water
- 3 Medjool dates, pitted
- 1 vanilla bean, roughly chopped
- ½ tsp ground cinnamon

Method

1 Soak the hazelnuts and almonds in a bowl of water for at least an hour, but preferably overnight.

2 Rinse and drain the nuts, then put them in your blender. Pour in the water, and add the dates, vanilla and cinnamon.

3 Cover and blend continuously until smooth.

4 If you have a nut milk bag, pour the blended mixture into it and hold over a bowl while you squeeze the bottom of the bag to release the milk. Otherwise use a muslin square or tea towel, or just use a sieve and press down with the back of a spoon. Set the pulp aside to use elsewhere, or discard.

5 Wash the blender and pour the freshly released milk back in. Give it another whiz, then pour into glasses and drink.

6 Or you can store in the fridge, in an airtight container for up to 3 days - just shake it up before you serve.

Chefs Note....

You can either drink this as a nourishing smoothie, or use it in coffee or tea, or on breakfast cereal etc.

SERVES 1

Kale and Green Tea Smoothie

Time to try... VEGAN

Ingredients

- 250ml/1 cup green tea
- 1 tsp freshly squeezed lemon juice
- 1 cucumber, roughly chopped
- 200g/7oz kale, stems removed
- ½ honeydew melon, seeds removed, flesh cut from the skin & cubed
- ½ tsp freshly grated ginger

Method

1 Pour the green tea and lemon juice into your blender. Add the cucumber, kale and melon. Sprinkle on the ginger.

2 Cover and blend on High until completely smooth.

3 Pour into a tall glass and drink.

Chefs Note....

Green tea contains lots of vitamins, calcium, zinc and iron. Taken with all the goodness of kale, and the melon, this is a healthy and energy-boosting smoothie – and tasty too! Feel free to add or substitute other vegetables, e.g. spinach for the kale.

SERVES 2

Almond and Banana Smoothie

Time to try...
VEGAN

Ingredients

- 500ml/2 cups almond milk
- 1 tsp pure vanilla extract
- 3 ripe bananas, each broken into 3 pieces
- 1 tbsp maca powder
- 1 tbsp chia seeds
- 1 tsp hemp seeds
- 25g/1oz cacao nibs
- Pinch salt
- A few goji berries, to garnish

Method

1 Pour the almond milk and vanilla extract into your blender. Add the banana, maca, chia seeds, hemp seeds and cacao nibs, with a pinch of salt.

2 Cover and blend on High until smooth.

3 Pour into 2 glasses, and garnish with the goji berries.

Chefs Note....

This delicious smoothie provides a big energy hit between meals. Goji berries supply extra vitamin C, zinc and antioxidants.

SERVES 2

Acai and Strawberry Smoothie

Time to try... VEGAN

Ingredients

- 250ml/1 cup freshly squeezed orange juice
- 100g/3½oz acai fruit puree
- 1 banana, broken into 3 pieces
- 200g/7oz fresh or frozen strawberries
- 1 tbsp chia seeds
- A few ice cubes

Method

1. Pour the orange juice and acai fruit puree into your blender. Add the banana, strawberries and chia seeds. Top with a few ice cubes if you wish.
2. Cover and blend on High into a smooth puree.
3. Pour into 2 tall glasses and drink.

Chefs Note....

Acai berries will give you a protein hit, while strawberries are packed with vitamin C and antioxidants.

SERVES 2

Strawberry Chocolate Smoothie

Time to try...
VEGAN

Ingredients

- 500ml/2 cups unsweetened vanilla soy milk
- 2 tbsp almond butter
- 2 sliced, frozen bananas
- 75g/3oz fresh or frozen strawberries
- 1 handful spinach
- 3 tbsp cocoa powder
- 1 tbsp flax seeds
- A few ice cubes

Method

1 Pour the soy milk into your blender. Add the almond butter, fruit and spinach. Sprinkle in the cocoa and flax seeds, and drop a few ice cubes on top.

2 Cover and blend until smooth.

3 Taste, and if necessary, add a little more cocoa powder or a liquid sweetener like agave nectar, and blend again.

4 Pour into 2 glasses and serve.

Chefs Note....

If you prefer, use almond or coconut milk instead of soy. Try also with blueberries instead of strawberries and kale instead of spinach. It will still be deliciously chocolatey and nutritious.

10

Tasty DESSERTS

Time to try....

VEGAN

SERVES 4

Ice Cream & Strawberry Sauce

Time to try...
VEGAN

Ingredients

- 5 chopped, frozen bananas
- 75g/3Oz pistachio nuts, + extra to garnish
- 1 tbsp of chia seeds, + extra to garnish
- 3 tbsp almond milk
- 1 tsp maple syrup, + 2 tsp
- 400g/14oz strawberries, chopped, + extra to garnish
- 250ml/1 cup water
- 2 tsp of maple syrup

Method

1 In a food processor or blender, blend together the frozen bananas, almond milk, 1 tsp maple syrup, the pistachio nuts and the chia seeds until it's the consistency of ice cream. Refrigerate to keep cool.

2 In a saucepan, gently heat the strawberries, water and remaining maple syrup until the strawberries are soft. Tip the contents into your blender and blend into a puree.

3 Return the mixture to the pan and increase the heat until the sauce reduces.

4 Pour it out into a bowl and refrigerate to cool and thicken.

5 Divide the ice cream between 4 dessert dishes. Pour the strawberry sauce over the top and garnish with extra strawberry halves, pistachio nuts and chia seeds.

Chefs Note....

A delightful non-dairy dessert to satisfy your sweet tooth. Plus, strawberries are packed with antioxidants and vitamin C, so it's good for you!

Cheesecake

SERVES 4+

Time to try... VEGAN

Ingredients

- 200g/7oz whole grain flour
- 2 tbsp sugar
- 1 tbsp whole wheat bran
- 1 tsp unsweetened cocoa powder
- ½ tsp ground cinnamon
- 60ml/¼ cup coconut oil, melted
- 1 tbsp maple syrup
- 700g/1lb 9oz silken extra-firm tofu
- 250ml/1 cup apple juice
- 150g/5oz sugar
- 1 tbsp agar flakes
- 1 tbsp lemon juice
- 1 tbsp vanilla extract
- Topping of your choice

Method

1 Preheat the oven to 180C/350F?Gas4

2 In a bowl, mix together the flour, sugar, bran, cocoa and cinnamon. Stir in the coconut oil and maple syrup. Turn the mixture out into the cake tin and press firmly to spread and compact the crust evenly.

3 Bake in the oven for 15 to 20 minutes, until golden brown. Remove from the oven and allow to cool completely.

4 Meanwhile, in a pan, heat the apple juice, sugar and agar flakes. Bring to the boil, lower the heat and cook for about 5 minutes, stirring occasionally, until the agar flakes are completely dissolved. Set aside and keep warm.

5 In a food processor, blend the tofu until completely smooth. Pour in the apple juice mixture, lemon juice and vanilla, and blend into a puree. Pour it over the baked crust. Leave to cool to room temperature and then chill in the fridge for at least 8 hours, until the filling has set.

6 When set, extract the cake by running a knife around the edges and releasing the spring. Spread on the topping of your choice. Slice and serve chilled.

SERVES 4

Tropical Pineapple Sorbet

Time to try... VEGAN

Ingredients

- 1 fresh pineapple, peeled, cored & chopped
- Juice & zest of 1 lime
- ½ tsp freshly grated ginger
- 75g/3oz caster sugar
- 1 tbsp fresh basil leaves, + a few extra to garnish
- 250ml/1 cup water

Method

1 Begin the day before you plan to serve the sorbet.

2 Combine all the ingredients in your blender, and blitz until smooth. Pour it into a freezer-proof container and freeze overnight.

3 The following day, remove it and allow to defrost slightly so it slides out of the container in a block. Chop the block into chunks that your blender can handle, and blitz again to make a thick, slushy purée. Pour this back into the freezer-proof container and freeze again for about an hour, until the sorbet can be scooped out.

4 Scoop the sorbet into chilled glasses and garnish with the extra basil leaves.

Chefs Note....

To add a little tropical zing, serve drizzled with white rum.

SERVES 4+

Chocolate Tart

Time to try... VEGAN

Ingredients

- 100g/3½oz coconut oil, melted
- 200g/7oz whole wheat vegan digestive biscuits, broken into small pieces
- 50g/2oz almonds
- 500g/1lb2oz vegan plain chocolate, chopped
- 700g/1lb9oz silken tofu, drained
- 2 tsp vanilla extract

Method

1 Preheat your oven to 200C/400F/Gas6.

2 Add the coconut oil, biscuits and almonds to your food processor. Pulse into coarse crumbs. Scrape the crumbs out into a pie dish, and press them down into the bottom of the dish to make a compact base.

3 Bake in the oven for 15 minutes, or until golden. Then remove and leave the base to cool for 15 minutes.Meanwhile, clean the food processor for later.

4 Melt the chocolate in a bowl over boiling water. Scrape it out into your food processor. Add the tofu and vanilla extract and blend until smooth, scraping down the sides as necessary.

5 Pour the chocolate mixture into the prepared base. Chill in the fridge for at least 4 hours before serving.

Chefs Note....

Serve with a scoop of vegan ice cream, if you wish.

Lemon Cake

SERVES 4+

Time to try...
VEGAN

Ingredients

- 250g/9oz vegan margarine
- 200g/7oz sugar
- 2 tsp vanilla extract
- 25g/1oz soya flour
- ½ tsp xanthan gum
- Juice & zest of 3 lemons
- 175ml/6floz warm water
- 150g/5oz plain flour
- 100g/3½oz corn flour
- 1 tbsp baking powder
- 50g/2oz ground almonds
- 150g/5oz icing sugar

Method

1 Preheat the oven to 180C/350F/Gas4. Line and grease a 30cm cake tin.

2 In a bowl, or food mixer, mix together the margarine, sugar, vanilla, soya flour, lemon zest and xanthan gum. Gradually stir in the two thirds of the lemon juice and all the water until the mixture is creamy.

3 Sieve the plain flour, corn flour and baking powder into the bowl and fold in gently.

4 Turn the mixture into the cake tin, and bake in the oven for 1-1¼hours, until the cake is golden and a skewer comes out clean.

5 In a small bowl stir together the icing sugar, lemon zest and the rest of the lemon juice. When the cake is cool, spread this lemon icing over the top. Leave to set and then slice and serve.

Chefs Note....

Although margarine is made from vegetable oil, most does in fact contain trace animal product, so you might want to check the labels before you buy.

SERVES 1

Nutty Chocolate Ice Cream

Time to try... VEGAN

Ingredients

- 2 sliced, frozen bananas
- 2 tbsp natural peanut butter
- 3 tbsp cacao nibs + a few more for garnish
- Pinch sea salt
- 1 tsp maple syrup
- Sprig of fresh mint, to garnish

Method

1. Use a food processor to whizz up the frozen banana slices into a crumb like consistency.
2. Add the peanut butter, cacao nibs, salt and maple syrup, and blend into a soft cream.
3. Serve in a chilled glass sprinkled with a few cacao nibs or chocolate chips and garnished with a mint sprig.

Chefs Note....
Try also with other nut butters, e.g. almond or hazelnut, and you can substitute vegan chocolate chips for the cacao nibs.

Eton Mess

SERVES 4

Time to try...
VEGAN

Ingredients

- Aquafaba from a 400g/14oz tinned chickpeas
- 100g/3½oz caster sugar
- 500g/1lb2oz mixed berries
- 2 tbsp icing sugar
- ½ tbsp rose water
- 400ml/14floz vegan coconut yogurt

Method

1 Pre-heat the oven to 140C/275F/Gas1. Line a baking tray with parchment.

2 Using an electric mixer whisk the aquafaba until white and fluffy. Gradually whisk in the caster sugar until the mixture forms stiff peaks, like making meringues.

3 Spoon the mixture onto the lined baking tray in dollops, and bake in the oven for 1½ hours, or until the meringues lift easily off the parchment. Allow them to cool.

4 Meanwhile, in a bowl, mix the berries with the icing sugar and rose water. Leave for half an hour to let the flavours infuse.

5 Pour the yogurt into a large bowl. Crumble the cooled 'meringues' over the top and stir. Then fold in about a third of the berries, to make a ripple effect in the yogurt. Divide the mixture between 4 glass serving dishes. Spoon the remaining berries over the top.

6 Serve at once, or chill in the fridge until you're ready to eat.

Chefs Note....

Aquafaba, the liquid from tinned chickpeas, is a useful egg substitute.

SERVES 2

Chocolate Mousse

Time to try...
VEGAN

Ingredients

- 100g/3½oz vegan cooking chocolate, roughly chopped
- 4 tbsp coconut cream
- 1 ripe avocado, peeled, stoned & roughly chopped
- ½ tsp vanilla extract
- 1 pinch sea salt
- 3 tbsp agave nectar
- 1 tsp orange zest

Method

1 In a glass bowl gently melt the chocolate over a pan of boiling water.

2 Remove from the heat and stir in the coconut milk until smooth.

3 When it's cooled, pour the mixture into your food processor or blender. Add the avocado, vanilla, salt, agave and orange zest. Blend until completely smooth and creamy.

4 Spoon into dessert glasses and chill in the fridge until you're ready to eat.

5 Serve garnished with a sprinkling of chopped nuts and a sprig of mint.

Chefs Note....
If you don't have coconut cream use the thickest, creamiest part of coconut milk which is found at the top of the tin.

Poached Plums

SERVES 4

Time to try...
VEGAN

Ingredients

- 500g/1lb2oz plums, stoned & quartered
- 250ml/1 cup water
- 200g/7oz caster sugar
- 1 cinnamon stick
- 1 vanilla pod, split, seeds scraped from out

Method

1 Pour the sugar and water into a pan. Add the cinnamon stick and vanilla. Gently heat until the sugar dissolves.

2 Add the plums and bring to the boil, then reduce the heat and leave to simmer for 5-10 minutes, until the plums are soft.

3 Leave to cool slightly. Pick out the cinnamon stick and vanilla pod, and serve into dessert dishes with a scoop of ice cream or coconut cream.

Chefs Note....
A lovely, warming dessert for autumn and winter. Plus, plums are packed with vitamins, calcium and zinc.

SERVES 4

Sherry Trifle

Time to try...
VEGAN

Ingredients

- 400g/14floz tin coconut milk (refrigerated)
- 100g/3½oz vegan margarine
- 150g/5oz golden caster sugar
- 200g/7oz self-raising flour
- 200ml/7floz almond milk, + more for the second jelly
- 1 tsp baking powder
- Dash of sherry or brandy
- 2 packets vegan jelly
- 225g/8oz fresh or frozen raspberries
- 1lt/4 cups vegan custard

Method

1 From a refrigerated can of coconut milk, pour away the thick clear liquid which has separated to the top. Pour the remaining white coconut milk into a bowl. Whisk it until it's smooth and thick. Set aside in the fridge.

2 Preheat the oven to 180C/350F/Gas4.

3 In a bowl, whisk together the margarine, caster sugar, flour, baking powder and almond milk. Turn it out into a Pyrex or other oven-proof bowl. Bake the sponge in the oven for around 30 minutes until it's golden on top and a skewer comes out clean.

4 While the sponge cools, prick it several times with a fork and pour a little sherry or brandy over it.

5 When the cake is cool, make up 1 jelly according to the packet instructions. Pour it over the sponge, then put the bowl in the fridge until the jelly sets.

6 Make up the other jelly using only a little hot water to melt the crystals, then use almond milk instead of water to make it up to size. Put the bowl back in the fridge to set.

7 When it is set, spread the raspberries over the top.

8 Make up the custard, and when it's cool, smooth it over the fruit. Refrigerate once more.

9 When the custard is set, spoon the thick coconut cream over the top, and serve.

CookNation

Other CookNation titles

If you enjoyed 'Time to try... VEGAN' you may also enjoy other books from CookNation including:

'Time to try... the FAST DIET'

'Time to try...the BLOOD SUGAR DIET"

and the extensive calorie counted 'Skinny' range of books.

To browse the full catalogue visit
www.bellmackenzie.com

26638819R10055

Printed in Great Britain
by Amazon